MW01247390

Your Kidmin Team

How to Recruit, Train and Retain Your Volunteers

LARRY HILLMAN

****

26 25 24 23 22 21 8 7 6 5 4 3 2 1

Your Kidmin Team

Library of Congress Cataloging-in-Publication Data:

ISBN:

Printed in the United States

****

CONTENTS

Endorsements

Larry Hillman is the real deal!

Jim Wideman, Kidmin & Family Ministry Pioneer

Larry Hillman is a children's ministry guru.

Roger Fields, Prez of Kidz Blitz

Foreword

I t has been said: if you want to go fast, go alone: if you want to go far, go together.

When I started in children's ministry I was a lone wolf. I did everything by myself. It wasn't that I didn't want any help, or that I thought that no one was as good as I was, I just didn't know the importance of building a team.

Over the course of my ministry I have observed and learned just how valuable it is to have a strong Ministry Team. It takes a lot work and dedication to build a team. It is always easier and faster to do something by yourself than it is to teach someone else to work with you. However, I found that I could only do so much by myself. I needed help to be more effective and to reach more children for Jesus. To do that, I needed to learn how to build a team.

Outside of prayer and God's anointing, recruiting, training and retaining a strong effective ministry team is the most important thing you can do when ministering to people of any age. This book will hopefully give you some ideas and insights into how to do just that.

RECRUITING

I. Pray

We have heard that we should pray so often that for many of us it goes in one ear and out the other. But saying we should pray is much more than just a cliché. Prayer goes ahead and prepares the way. Prayer will enlighten your spirit to see what God has instore for you and your team. Prayer will touch the heart of those who God has anointed to help you.

Spend time praying to gain insight and direction on who to recruit, when to recruit and how to recruit. When you go to God in prayer, do so knowing and expecting Him to meet your need. And your need is for helpers to spread the Gospel.

And my God will meet all your needs according
to the riches of his glory in Christ Jesus.
Philippians 4:19 NIV

Is there anything that is more dear to the heart of God than spreading the Gospel to those that Jesus died for?

Ask the Lord of the harvest, therefore, to
send out workers into his harvest field
Matthew 9:38 NIV

All of us want more workers, but remember, you don't just want any worker. You want someone dedicated to serving God and children. So ask the Holy Spirit to direct you to those who are supposed to be a part of your team. The best workers you will ever have are those who are God sent.

II. Have a plan

Have you ever really thought about how you recruit? Is it just something you do once in a while without any real thought going into it? Do you have a standard recruiting pitch that you use? Or do you just plead and beg for someone to help out when you are short of workers.

Good recruiters have a plan. They have a standard verbal pitch that is designed to excite people to join their team. Check out the military recruiters. They have a prepared sales pitch, a list of all the benefits of joining, a list of job assignments, a list of possible promotions, posters and volunteer forms ready to be filled out.

If you want to be a successful recruiter, you must have a plan.

Where there is no vision, the people
perish Proverbs 28:19 KJV

One of the most important things you can share with a potential worker is why you do what you are doing. Share with them that approximately 85% of everyone who is serving Jesus became a Christian between the ages of 4 and 14, - the majority of them are before the age of 12. Tell them stories of seeing children accept Christ into their life, and how their behavior changed. Tell them how they now have a smile and how it seems that their face is beaming with the love of Jesus.

People will join your team because they see the significance of your ministry. People need to know the why, before they know the what. So spend some time telling them the why, before telling them what they will do.

Show them where your ministry is now, what you are doing to reach children and involve their parents. Tell them why you sing certain songs and why you utilize object lessons or puppets and why other parts of your service are in place. Then show them where you want to go, and explain that they are an integral part of you fulfilling God's plan for this ministry.

Next always have a volunteer application ready to give to potential workers. You are much more successful when you strike when the iron is hot, rather than coming back a few days later after things have cooled down. Have that application ready and have them fill it out now.

III. Job Description/Procedures

How does having a list of job descriptions help you recruit? Well, ask yourself this question. Would you take a job if you didn't know what it entailed? Most people think they will be asked to stand in front of a group and teach, or lead, because that's what they see you do. Well, let me tell you, most people are very reluctant to stand in front of a group of people and teach or lead. In fact public speaking is the number one fear of adults in America. By showing potential recruits a list of available jobs, it allows them to rest easy in knowing that they will not be expected to teach or lead from the stage. (A list of my job descriptions is in the Appendix.)

There are many people who have gifts and talents that are best applied off stage. You need these gifted people to help you present the Gospel in an entertaining and professional manner. In order to get them to join your team, you must be able to show them that you have a job and a place for them to use their talents.

Another major hurdle you must overcome is people's fear of commitment. Most people subconsciously think that when they join the children's ministry team, they are committing for a lifetime. They think they will be stuck forever, and most aren't ready to make such a commitment. So to overcome this fear, have an ending date for them. Let them know that they are only agreeing to serve for three months, or six months. After that they can decide to stay with your team, or be free to leave. Having a firm ending date will put your potential volunteers at ease and make them much more likely to make a short-term commitment.

IV. How did Jesus recruit?

Here are three times Jesus recruited people for his team.

As Jesus was walking beside the Sea of Galilee, he saw two brothers, Simon called Peter and his brother Andrew. They were casting a net into the lake, for they were fishermen. [19] *"Come, follow me," Jesus said, "and I will send you out to fish for people."* [20] *At once they left their nets and followed him.* [21] *Going on from there, he saw two other brothers, James son of Zebedee and his brother John. They were in a boat with their father Zebedee, preparing their nets. Jesus called them,* [22] *and immediately they left the boat and their father and followed him.*

Matthew 4:18-22

As Jesus went on from there, he saw a man named Matthew sitting at the tax collector's booth. "Follow me," he told him, and Matthew got up and followed him.

Matthew 9:9

The next day Jesus decided to leave for Galilee.
Finding Philip, he said to him, "Follow me."

John 1:34

What can we learn from the style, method or process Jesus used to recruit?

1. Jesus didn't beg.

Jesus had prayed for workers and he believed his prayer would be answered. He had prayed for God to give those that were to be on his team a desire to join and serve. Jesus knew that God already knew who should be on his team. So he asked God to show him who they were. So after Jesus knew who God wanted on his team, he simply invited them to come join the team.

There was no asking or pleading or "please help us we need so much help." No, Jesus didn't make his recruiting pitch about him and his ministry. He made it about the recruit fulfilling the desire that God had placed in their heart. So, when Jesus said, "Follow me," they were more than ready to follow because they knew it would complete the call that God had put in their hearts.

2. Jesus wasn't afraid to ask.

Don't be afraid to ask people to join your team. The absolute worst they can do is say no. Don't assume people don't want to help. Don't start by apologizing. There are many people looking for a way to serve, they just need someone to give them an opportunity.

3. Jesus recruited one-on-one.

Notice in the aforementioned recruiting anecdotes that Jesus, recruited one at a time. I know there were two brothers, but his words touched each one individually. It was a personal invitation, not a general announcement or appeal to a large group.

Also notice Jesus wasn't recruiting people just to serve others. Jesus called them called them to follow him. When you ask people to join a team you are leading you are in essence asking them to follow you. Since this is the case, you need to make sure your life is one that people would want to follow. How you dress, how you talk, your attitude, personality and commitment to God and your church will be front and center to someone you are recruiting. Live your life in such a way that others will want to follow you.

Here is a list of things that might be helpful when recruiting.

- Make volunteer opportunities clear and accessible
- Be specific about what you need
- Give people a chance to try it out
- Seek out past volunteers
- Offer simple sign-up
- Offer a volunteer/sign-up day church-wide
- Volunteer page on your website
- Volunteers featured on web or Facebook or another platform
- Get current volunteers to recruit

V. Where to find workers

Let's first look at some things that don't work.

- A notice in the weekly announcement sheet
- A flyer on the bulletin board
- Announcement from the pulpit
- Sending out postcards
- Crying and begging

Now let's look at what does work.

- Personal invitation
- It doesn't have to be you inviting, it can be someone on your team
- Recruit people you have a personal relationship with
- Remember, people are following you
- Share past victories or testimonies with recruits
- Connect them to your, "Why"

VI. Keep your standards high

You want the very best people on your team. Don't recruit by telling people that what they will be doing is not that big of a deal. Or that it is really simple and won't require that much of their time. When you do this, you get exactly what you are recruiting. You get workers that don't really care because what they are doing is, "no big deal." You get workers who don't put in time preparing because, "you can do this job without a lot of preparation." You get workers who show up late, if at all, because once again, what they are doing is, "no big deal."

So, while you don't want to scare people away by saying this is the toughest, hardest thing you will ever do, you do want to let them know they are taking on a job that is very important. Tell them that they will have to be on time, prayed up and prepared to do their job. If they absolutely must miss a time/service they are scheduled for, require them to follow your procedure for that situation.

Have a checklist that mirrors their job description. Ask that they check-off this list after every service and place it in a specified location. People need to be constantly reminded of their responsibility and the importance of doing their job with excellence. This checklist is one way of doing that. Also on Monday or Tuesday, thank them for filling out this list, or gently remind them that you didn't get their checklist. They have to know you are looking at it if you want them to fill it out.

Another way of keeping your standards high is complimenting people for doing a good job, but also calling them out when they don't do a good job. Correction should, when possible, always be done in private. It should also be done in a way that is meant to help your worker, not demean your worker. I've found the best way to correct is just by asking questions: Why did you do it that way. Or why did you not do it that way? If they have a good reason, don't be afraid to accept it and move on. If not, remind them of why they are doing their job and the importance of their job. Remember they are volunteers, so always be kind and patient. But also don't be afraid to hold them to your standard or even remove them if nothing changes after you have spoken to them several times.

You can find a place for everyone, and remember, not everyone needs to be on stage.

TRAINING

Communication is EVERYTHING

T he first part of this chapter is about communication and leading. I believe that as a leader, everything you do is training your workers. You are training them by what and how you communicate, your tone of voice, your being early, your attention to detail, the way you treat people, how you hold them to your standards. You also train by being late, not attending the adult service, or not following procedures.

In short, the way you do your job is training your workers how they should do their job.

The most important component of training, is communication. If you tell someone how to do something and they do not understand what you said, you have just wasted their time and yours.

The best advice on communication I ever heard was: Communicate until you think you have communicated way too much, then communicate some more.

Let's begin with what does the Bible does say about communication.

My dear brothers and sisters, take note of this:
Everyone should be quick to listen, slow to speak
and slow to become angry. James 1:19 NIV

I. Be a good listener

In order to be a good leader, we need to be good listeners. I mean, really listen. Here are two things that will help you become a good listener.

1. Ask questions, don't assume.

   Make sure you understand what they are saying. We all have a different point of view and yours may not be the same as theirs. Clarify what is being said by digging a little deeper with a couple of questions.

2. Paraphrase their statement back to them.

   Example: Worker: "I am doing twice as much work as the worker stationed on the other side of the room. They just walk around doing nothing and I get left correcting the children and handing out the worksheets and stuff."

You: "So what you are saying is that Bob isn't doing his share of the work?"

Worker: "Yes, and that makes my job much harder."

You: "So you want Bob to do his share?

I know this sounds like stating the obvious, but it really does work. You can use this technique with, children, workers, angry parents or anyone for that matter..

When you paraphrase it calms people down because it forces them to think about what you said. We all know a calm logical person is much better to deal with than an emotional person. Paraphrasing causes them to change from looking at the situation emotionally, to logically. It also shows them that you understand their concern and are aware of how they feel. I've used it many, many times and it really does change things quickly to a calmer softer conversation.

II. Good communication will build trust and relationships.

When you consistently communicate the same message under all conditions, it builds trust. People aren't afraid to make a decision because they know exactly what the leader would do if they were faced with the same decision.

Trust goes both ways. The leader must trust their worker, but the worker must also trust the leader. All relationships are built on trust. Here are some things a leader can do to build trust.

- Keep your word
- Follow the procedures you require of others
- Don't promise something you can't deliver
- Allow for workers to fail
- Don't get angry, yell or embarrass a worker in front of others
- Give real specific compliments, not just general compliments
- Don't be afraid to say, "I blew it."
- Be willing to let others receive the applause
- Be willing to accept new ideas

Here are a couple of stories highlighting instances of bad communication.

I was playing softball and the ball was hit over my head. On this field, the right field fence was very close as the park had moved the fence in and added some basketball courts. As I turned and ran toward the fence the centerfielder was yelling, "NO FENCE!" We had shouted this to each other many times. What it meant was there is no fence for you to worry about. So, I trusted him and continued following the ball. Just as the ball hit my glove, I ran face-first, into the fence. Fortunately, it was a chain-link fence which only bounced me backward to the ground and caused me to drop the ball. I jumped up, threw the ball to 2nd base and turned toward my centerfielder and yelled, "No fence?" I wasn't so quick to listen to him the next time.

I was the 3rd base coach on a girls' slow pitch softball team. I only had two signs for the batters when it came to swinging or taking a pitch. The signal to swing was both arms extended straight down by my side down, the signal to not swing was when I crossed arms. The count was 3 balls and 2 strikes, and none of the pitches had been close to being a strike. The batter had swung and missed twice at pitches way out of the strike zone to acquire the 2 strikes. I looked straight into the batter's eyes, I lifted my arms up and crossed them before lowering them onto my chest. The batter nodded her head, acknowledging she had the sign. The pitch came in very high and the batter jumped off the ground to swing at a pitch over her head for strike 3. As we walked back to the dugout I asked her, "Didn't you see the no swing sign?" She said, "Oh, I thought that was the signal to swing." Obviously, I had not clearly communicated my signals.

III Hands on training

Here are the steps I follow when bringing on a new team member.

1. Take 5

   A leader or experienced team member gives the new team member a quick tour of the children's area explaining the what's and how's and answering any questions.

2. On-the-job training

   The new team member is paired up with an experienced team member. The new team member shadows the experienced team member during a service. This may happen one, two or three times, depending on the complexity of the job. After each service they fill out the check sheet together.

3. Follow-up meeting

   When the experienced team member believes the new team member is ready, the leader sets up a meeting with the new team member. The leader gets feedback from the worker and makes sure that the worker is comfortable with their commitment to the team.

4. Job assignment/description

   At the follow-up meeting, the new team member is officially assigned a job and the leader covers the job description with the new team member.

5. Check list

   The leader explains the Check Sheet. Each job has a Service Check Sheet. This sheet mirrors the job descriptions, but not in as much detail. It is a simple bullet list of responsibilities. At the end of each service the responsibilities are checked off as completed, dated, signed and left in the assigned place.

6. Feedback

    It is important as a leader to encourage feedback; positive and negative. The leader will touch base with each new team member after they have served for three months. Also the leader will encourage them to reach out by text, email or in person to give feedback for the entire time they are on the team.

7. Quarterly meeting

    Once a quarter have a team meeting. You may have to have the same meeting twice as some may be able to attend at one time and not another. Zoom meeting may be the best and easiest way to stay in touch.

IV. Meetings

Make your meeting upbeat, friendly and valuable. Don't have a meeting just to have a meeting, make it worth their time. I once went to a school faculty meeting where the principal looked around, picked up a book from a student's desk, randomly opened to a page and read a paragraph. He then put the book down, looked at the faculty and said, "Well, that's about all I have to say today, that's the end of our meeting." I remember being irate that someone would waste my time for something so useless. If you don't have anything to say then don't have a meeting.

Have a written agenda or schedule. People like to know what to expect. Pass out the agenda a day or two early, and then STICK to it. Nothing loses credibility like saying you are going to do something and then not sticking to it.

On the other hand, building and keeping trust works wonders. It has been proven in many studies that people will work harder and longer for someone they trust.

One hour is the absolute longest you should meet. You will have already lost most of them long before that. Remember, you don't need long meetings, you need effective meetings.

Serve refreshments, have a time of sharing, and encourage friendships. Give them a takeaway from the meeting, maybe a hand out or a new idea to ponder. Make them a part of what is happening so they have ownership in the ministry.

Avoid hallway meetings, or Sunday morning meetings. Information passed in the hallway is usually forgotten. When your mind is focused on something, you are on a mission, so when somebody tells you something, you say "OK," and walk on, still thinking about your mission. What they said is totally lost. So, don't have meeting in the hallway or on Sunday mornings when everyone is busy serving others, they just don't work.

Always start and end your meeting with prayer.

V. Don't forget your body language.

Many times, our actions communicate more than our words. It is not always what we say, but how we say it.

Be aware of:

1. Facial expressions

2. Tone of voice

3. Leaning toward or away

4. Sitting higher denotes authority

5. Crossed arms shows you are shutting them out

6. If you are having a one-on-one meeting, laying a pencil pointed toward either party is open and friendly. However, laying that pencil pointed sideways says they are approaching a line that should not be crossed.

In an article titled, "The Importance of Effective Communication," published by Stevenson University, it states:

Nonverbal cues are so strong because they communicate to others on a subconscious level, causing individuals to regard nonverbal communication as, true, communication.

When verbal language and body language are congruent, this works to enhance the overall quality of the message. On the opposite end of the spectrum, there can also be a sense of mistrust developed when body language does not match up to what is being verbalized.

RETAINING

I. Develop a personal relationship

People will work "with" someone harder and longer than they will work "for" someone. Get to know your volunteers. Have lunch with them after church or during the week if possible. Learn their interests and hobbies. Nothing makes a person feel better than talking about themselves and their interests.

One of my workers loves football - college and professional. Each time she works, I make a point of asking her about a game that just happened or one coming up. That's all I have to do and she takes the ball and runs with it. She talks and talks and it makes her feel like someone is interested in her, not just in what she does. This volunteer has now worked with me for almost 20 years!

Learn when your workers' birthdays and anniversaries are and send them a card to mark each occasion. Learn the names of their family members and ask about them regularly. Keep in touch regularly with email and text. Just a short thank you, or asking if they have any questions or concerns will do.

Let them know just how much you see in them. Compliment them often and thank them for what they do. They need to know that you believe in them and see more in them than they see in themselves.

Nothing builds loyalty and commitment as strongly as a relationship between friends, someone you know has your best interest at heart. A friend will have your back, and will defend you and fight for you.

II. Regular communication

People like to be informed. People like to be appreciated. People don't like to be taken for granted. You can accomplish the first two and avoid the third with just a little bit of communication.

In your calendar, have a regularly scheduled time to reach out to your volunteers. A reminder pops up every Tuesday at 10am on my computer screen. It reminds me to send an email out to those who served on the previous weekend. I always thank them for their commitment and then I add in something specific that they did. This lets them know that I'm paying attention and not just sending a generic email.

If for some reason a worker misses their scheduled time to serve, I reach out to them as soon as possible after the service to let them know that they were missed. I try to call, but I'll text or email if I have to. In my call, email or text I express a concern for them by asking if something happened that caused them to miss their scheduled time to serve. I tell them that I am very aware of how hard they try to always serve and if I need to pray with them about something I'm happy to do so. Most times they answer with a simple I forgot, or I had family stop by or something like that.

I then say, OK, but next time if you could reach out to a team member and ask them to cover for you it would really help. What you do is a big part of our serving the children and also we really like you and were concerned when you didn't show up.

By doing this, your purpose and accomplishment is three-fold: you hold them accountable, let them know that what they do is important, and let them know that you care about them. Everything about your call to them was supportive and positive, but they will try very hard to not get another call like that.

Have a regularly scheduled meeting or Zoom meeting. This could be once every two months or once a quarter. When you have your meeting, share your vision, map out what you see in the future and include them in your planning. Having them help with the planning, and the implementing of your plans, helps them to buy into the plan and gives them an ownership stake in the ministry. Everyone wants to be a part of a team, all for one and one for all. No one wants to work for a dictator.

One time I was working at a school as a special needs resource teacher. My job was to work with students who had been identified as needing more help to complete their schoolwork. I would pick them up from their classroom and take them to my classroom where there were only three or four children. I could then give them more personal attention and help them accomplish their schoolwork. When a student needed a little extra motivation, we would create a chart of their daily work schedule. As the student finished their work, their teachers, -homeroom, coach, music, art, resource-would check it off and sign the chart. This was a lot of work, and since I was the resource teacher, it was my job to create, monitor and file the completed charts. As you can guess, I only did this when it was really needed.

One day I was given a new student. Within a week my supervisor walked up to me and handed me a chart she had made for my new student. I was directed to make copies and begin monitoring and filing the completed charts. I looked at her and said, "No, you created it, you do it," and walked away.

She stood there in stunned silence as I walked away. I had never reacted in such a way before. In fact, I was known for doing the exact opposite. I was known for going the extra mile, helping when it wasn't my responsibility and doing whatever I was asked.

I did quickly walk back to her and say, "Okay, give me the sheet."

Why had I acted like that? I asked myself that question and I'll share with you what I shared with my supervisor a few days later. The problem was she had decided on all the skills the student should accomplish, how often the skills would be checked, what the reward was for accomplishing them and the consequences if they were not accomplished. She had decided all of that and then given me all the work to make sure it was done. I had all the responsibility and work, and no say-so on the creation of the chart. No say-so on what the skills were, what the reward was, how to carry out the punishment if not completed, just "Here, go do this extra work." If I had been asked to make a chart, or included in creating a chart, I would have felt like I was a part of what was going on. I would have been working with my supervisor, not just for a dictator.

If you want your volunteers to work with you and be a part of the ministry, then give them some say on what you are doing and how you do it.

III. Remind them of why you are serving

Keep the vision of your ministry before your workers. Put up posters with bullet points and email the vision several times a year to keep it front and center.

Make the vision personal. Tell them what you have planned for them, how they will help accomplish the vision. Let them know that they are a big part of the plans for the ministry. Share with them your vision of where you see them going and what you believe they are capable of accomplishing. Build up their self-esteem by giving them more access to your vision and planning. Make them a part of deciding the pathway forward for the ministry. Give them "ownership" of your future.

Constantly share testimonies of how people were blessed by your ministry and workers. Find success stories from parents and children and share them with everyone. Share these on your church website, and social media.

People will stay with you longer, work harder and be more loyal when they know why you are doing something, and not just the what.

IV. Celebrate

B e on the lookout for success stories, and share them with your team, your church and your pastor. Put your success stories on social media, or in an email, and make a big deal about it because it is a big deal. Remind them that what they just did, affected eternity.

Be constantly saying thank you to your workers. Remind them just how much you appreciate them and how much Jesus appreciates them. A little recognition of the time and effort they put in goes a long way.

Send them a card on their birthday, marriage anniversary, or the anniversary of when they began serving on your team.

Also, just like for the kids, do all you can to make serving on your team enjoyable. Talk with them, ask about their family or job. Call them every so often during the week, or meet a few team members for lunch. Do life together, not just church together.

And finally, remember that people do what is celebrated. They respond positively to praise and will work twice as hard for someone who celebrates their success.

APPENDIX

Job Descriptions

1. Greeter:

    <u>First service</u>: arrive on duty for huddle-up at 8:55.

    After huddle-up you are on duty.

    <u>Second service</u>: arrive for duty at 10:45.

    Stand by the front door.

    Greet all children with a handshake, a smile and by

    telling them you are glad to see them.

If this is their first time, give the parents the parent information sheet and introduce them to the check-in coach.

After they have checked in, escort the child into the classroom and introduce them to the crowd control coach.

Make sure returning children check in on the computer.

2. Check-in

First service: arrive on duty for huddle-up at 8:55.

After huddle-up you are on duty.

Second service: arrive for duty at 10:45.

Stand at the check-in station

Assist regular attenders with checking in on the computer.

Assist first time attenders in filling out the registration card.

Give each person dropping off a child the proper pick-up information.

3. Video Game

First service: arrive on duty for huddle-up at 8:55.

Second service: arrive for duty at 10:45.

Become familiar with the video games.

Upon entering the classroom, turn on the monitors and the video games.

As children arrive, help them with the video game of their choice.

Rotate the children when others are waiting for a turn to ensure that everyone gets a chance to play.

4. Media

    First service: arrive on duty for huddle-up at 8:55.

    Second service: arrive for duty at 10:45.

    Follow the checklist for turning on the sound and
    video equipment.

    As soon as possible turn on music to play before
    service starts.

    Check the order of service and run through the
    lineup to make sure everything works.

    First service: When children are dismissed, turn
    on the music.

    Second service: When children are dismissed,
    follow the checklist for turning off the sound
    and video equipment.

5. Crowd Control

    Arrive 15 minutes before service. Introduce yourself
    to new children and greet those you know. Spend
    time getting to know the children by asking
    about their school, home and interests. When it
    is time to start the service, encourage children to
    be seated and get ready for service. Once service
    starts please stand next to the children on the end
    of a row or behind the last row. When a child is
    being disruptive, quietly redirect their attention
    to the leader. Anytime you have to go in front
    of the children, remember to crouch down so as
    not to block the view of other children or take
    attention away from the leader. We ask children
    to remove hats and hoodies and to sit upright
    in their chair. When asked to stand, please
    encourage them to do so. If a child raises their

hand, please quietly go to them and ask what they need. They may go to the restroom but water is only allowed before or after the service. If they want to respond to something the leader is saying, please ask them to see the leader after the service. It is very important that we always talk to the children in a pleasant calm voice. If disruptive behavior continues after two or three interventions, please ask the child to move to another seat. If further actions are needed, please ask the leader for help.

6. Setup

Arrive at a predetermined time agreed upon by the leader. Set up the chairs with a center aisle: five chairs on each side in the front row and six in the back row.

7. Cleanup

   First Service: After children have been dismissed, pickup any trash on chairs or floor and check to see if the bathroom needs any attention.

   Second Service: After children have been dismissed, pickup any trash on chairs or floor and attend to the bathroom. Empty the trashcans located in the bathroom, by the water cooler and next to the media desk, into the large trashcan by the back door. Please replace the plastic liner in each trashcan.

8. Takedown

   Move all items and props used to the proper storage area.

9. Visitor Follow-up

    Address the first-time visitor postcard using the information on the registration card. Place a postcard stamp on the postcard and place it in the mail on Monday morning.

10. Praise and Worship Leader

    Pray for the service and for which songs for the children to sing. Practice song words and movements. Develop a team to assist you in leading. Determine a time to practice with your team. On Sunday, lead the children in praise and worship while always promoting Jesus and having fun.

11. Praise and Worship Team Member

    Assist the Praise and Worship Leader in leading the children in worship, whether singing or playing an instrument. Regularly pray for the service, attend practice sessions, and lead with joy and enthusiasm.

12. Object Lesson

Using information from leader, prepare an object lesson to be presented to the children. Always remember to prepare ahead of time and practice, practice, practice. When presenting the object lesson, remember to be loud, have large movements, this will keep their attention by being fast paced and make it fun.

13. Memory Verse Assistant:

Present the memory verse with Power Point, DVD or other chosen methods. Make it fun and show how it applies to their life.

14. Offering

Pray and receive the offering. Keep track of the winning team in the current format being used.

15. Assistant Leader

When the leader is not present, the assistant leader will take the position of leading the service. Using information from the leader, present the lesson for that week's service using the appropriate equipment and with the appropriate enthusiasm.

15. Security

<u>First service</u>: arrive on duty for huddle-up at 8:55.

<u>Second service</u>: arrive for duty at 10:45.

Your station will be at the entrance door of the classroom. With a smile and being very courteous, allow only the children and their parents or guardians to enter the classroom.

When service ends, only allow children to leave with an adult that presents the proper pick-up information.

16. Salvation Response

Take notice of the children who raise their hand to accept Jesus as their Savior.

Immediately following the salvation prayer, present each of these children with our

Salvation Information Sheet. Have them put their name on it and instruct them to give it to their parents. Also, add their name to the salvation list kept in the media booth.

(A copy of the Salvation Information Sheet is in the Appendix)

17. Follow-up

Address and stamp the FLC Kids postcard for each first-time attender. Mail the postcard on Monday. (A copy of the FLC Kids postcard is in the Appendix)

ABOUT THE AUTHOR

Larry began ministering to children at age 17. Since then Larry has led children's ministry almost every Sunday for over 45 years. He has conducted week long children's crusades, statewide children's meetings, national meetings, summer camp and even ministered at meetings internationally. Larry has a B.A. in Elementary Education, M.A. in Supervision/ Administration, and a B.A. in Special Education. He has worked as a Teacher in regular education and special education, Assistant Principal, Principal, and an Exceptional Student Education Specialist in church and public schools.

Larry has spoken at conferences, led leadership groups and authored several books.

Larry is married to his wife Jeanine, they have four grown children and six grandchildren.

Since 1998, Larry has been Associate/Children's Pastor at Faith Life Church in Tampa Florida and a Ministry Coach, Mentor and Speaker.

Find out more about Larry at <u>LarryHillmanMinistries.com</u>

Made in the USA
Columbia, SC
25 May 2023